Abraham - Father of Faith

By Michael Christian Bell

Copyright

ISBN-13: 978-1490461106

ISBN-10: 1490461108

Contents

Abram relinquishes his old way of life. 5

Abram's Call 9

Down to Egypt 11

Abram and Lot separate 15

Lot in Sodom 16

Melchizedek 19

Divine Rewards for Abram 20

Hagar and Ishmael 22

The Abrahamic Covenant 27

Visitation 31

Lot and his daughters 34

Abimelech and the Philistines 38

Isaac and Ishmael 41

Beersheba 46

Isaac sacrifice 49

Machpelah 53

Isaac's Bride 55

Keturah 58

Abraham's Eulogy 60

Chronology Chart/Bible Genealogical table* 61

3

Abram relinquishes his old way of life.

Inside the ancient metropolis of Ur, a prominent city of the Chaldeans lived a particular family headed by an old man called Terah, along with his sons Nahor, Abram and their wives. Terah and family naturally followed the religion of the Chaldeans in Ur - Joshua 24:2. However, at some period of time, Terah's son Abram experienced a crisis of faith. Why this occurred no one knows; however I can speculate and say that when his older brother Haran died, the grieving Abram began questioning the existence of the Chaldean gods.

It is evident that Abram had a religious encounter with a new Deity, and this incident brought about a life changing and revolutionary experience. Apparently, Abram even heard the voice of his new God, and his message challenged him. How long this new relationship had existed, whether recent or long term cannot be determined, but his new God had appeared to him and said:

"Get out of your country and away from your people and come into a land that I will show you"- Acts 7:2.

Understanding God's plan can be both a testing time and gradual process because Abram's initial call required a dismantling of his lifestyle and culture. Terah and his sons had lived comfortably as citizens of Ur; this can be observed by Abram's abundant possessions. Previously, the lifestyle of Ur had totally dominated his life, but his new God inspired him radically, and being influenced by the powerful and compelling beckoning, he made the crucial decision to follow the divine directions. Thus he migrated, taking his father Terah and nephew Lot, with him. Co-incidentally, they journeyed westward towards Haran, a city that bore the same name as his deceased brother.

Josephus, the ancient Jewish Historian and contemporary of Paul and John the Apostle, indicates that Terah consented to migrate because he grieved over the death of his son Haran and wanted to remove himself from anything that reminded him of his son. Haran was survived by three children: Lot, Milcah, and Iscah, whom Josephus identifies as Sarai. This potentially establishes Sarai as Abram's niece and not his sister, as is traditionally believed. Females were generally not listed in the genealogies, but Sarai and Milcah seemed important characters and the scriptures honor them because of their marriages to Terah's sons.

It seems more feasible that Abram married his niece rather than his half-sister. If Terah cared for her after the death of Haran, then she would naturally be considered a sister to Abram as he claimed when in Egypt.[1] Abraham indicated there that she was the daughter of his father, but from a different mother.[2] This agrees with the cultural thinking of those times because tribal patriarchs bore the title of Father. Also, Sarai was conspicuously called Terah's daughter-in-law in Genesis 11:31. This inclusion would not have been mentioned if she was indeed his actual daughter.

The trading city of Haran lay inland on the crossroads of Nineveh and Carchemish in the northern part of

---

[1] Genesis 12:13
[2] Genesis 20:12

what we call [3]Mesopotamia, by the river Belias. Initially the call came to Abram to forsake his country, family and way of life, and move to Canaan. But subconsciously shackled to his father, Abram only responded partially to the call; maybe the city of Haran seemed a congenial place to settle in. Eventually, Terah died at the lengthy and grand old age of two-hundred and five years. The lifespan of men had dramatically plummeted after the flood.

The rapid decline of human longevity was evidenced as follows:
Noah lived 600 years before the Deluge, and another 350 years after for a total lifespan of 950 years.
Shem reached 600 years: he produced his first child at 100 years of age; that was two years after the Flood.
Arphaxad lived 438 years: first child at 35 years.
Salah lived 433 years: first child at 30 years.
Eber lived 464 years: first child at 34 years.
Peleg lived 239 years: first child at 30 years.
Reu lived 239 years: first child at 32 years.
Serug lived 230 years: first child at 32 years.
Nahor lived 148 years: first child at 29 years.
Terah lived 205 years: first child at 70 years.

Terah produced Abram at the age of one hundred and thirty years. That was sixty years after Haran's birth.[4] The total period elapsed between the Flood and Abram's entry into Canaan, according to Shem's genealogical record, was four hundred and twenty nine years. Incidentally, Shem lived contemporary with

---

[3] A Greek word: meso – between or middle, and potamus – river; meaning 'between the rivers.'
(Mesopotamia is all the land located   between the Euphrates and Tigris.)
[4] Genesis 12:5

Methuselah for some ninety years before the Flood and also contemporary with Abram after the Flood for approximately seventy five years. Adding to that thought: Abraham lived for one hundred and seventy five years, making him contemporary with Jacob for fifteen years.[5]

Contemplating Shem's coexistence with Abram is not so astonishing: when I put these notes together a score of folk in New Zealand had reached the age of one hundred years and over. They were contemporary with nineteenth century life. Some Taranaki Maori from that same period massacred and ate the Chatham Islanders, known as Mori-Ori. In 1893, the majority of members of parliament were in favor of giving women the vote. In 1898, the old-age-pension was introduced. These folk were alive before Queen Victoria died; before the assassination of President McKinley; and before the Trans-Siberian railway opened. New Zealand had been a European colony for a trifling fifty years.

A child of ten years is capable of transmitting a vast store of information. The folk I mentioned had ten years of nineteenth century life experience in their memories. Shem possessed a rich knowledge that was sourced from a previous world. It should come as no surprise that the revelation and accounts of God's dealings with mankind were available in Abram's days because significant people who possessed direct knowledge of the Flood were still alive. Indeed, the Flood remained an accepted historical fact among the ancient civilizations. However, the truth of the account become distorted and confused as the different belief

---

[5] Genesis 25:7

systems emerged from the ruins of Nimrod's Babel. The population explosion and subsequent dispersion from Babel separated multitudes; naturally, dynamic links and relationships were sundered and people such as Shem, Japheth and Ham eventually became obscure to their offspring. In this world of the super highway of information, multitudes neither care nor have a clue who their ancestors were, particularly young people. Thus, family links and family knowledge are easily lost and forgotten permanently. When some people mature and search out their individual ancestry, they are profoundly affected by the stories that emerge from their ancestors. The picture that arises is how the previous generations failed to preserve family history. Fortunately, God has preserved the family tree of every man and woman, and most importantly, he preserved the ancestry of the Messiah Jesus – God incarnate in man. Melchizedek the priest of the Highest God also lived contemporary with Shem and Abram; whether contact existed between them can only be conjectured.

Abram's Call

Now the Lord had said unto Abram, "Get out of your country, and from your people, and from your father's house, unto a land that I will show you: And I will make you a great nation, and I will bless you, and make your name great; and you shall be a blessing: And I will bless them that bless you, and curse him that curses you: and in you shall all families of the earth be blessed.[6]"

At seventy-five years of age, the year that Terah died, Abram departed from Haran. Abram's obligation to his old man had finally terminated. The old man represents the carnal nature that dominates and controls our lives.

From Haran he journeyed to Shechem in Canaan. Three hundred miles is a moderate trip by today's standards, but definitely a long and hazardous journey in ancient times, and it entailed a radical break from conventional and cultural customs. Abram ventured into the unknown and the unfamiliar. However, he did not receive guidance from visible things; he received guidance from the invisible. He moved by faith and cut himself off completely from his old way of life; for him everything became new.

To change one's direction in life at seventy-five years of age is remarkable. Abram and Sarai were obviously more youthful than our average seventy-five year old person in modern times, but this is relative because there are many folk in their seventies and even eighties who retain good health and a youthful appearance.

Abram took Sarai his wife and Lot his brother's son and all their substance they had gathered and servants they acquired in Haran and they went forth to go into the land of Canaan and arrived there. Abram passed through the land until he reached Shechem and the plain of Moreh. And the Canaanites already lived in the land. [7]

---

[6] Genesis 12: 1-3
[7] Genesis 12:5-6.

The Canaanites[8] appear in scripture in their various tribes. Some were large in stature and others were apparently average in physique. They spread abroad with their borders reaching from Sidon to Gaza and then across to Sodom and Gomorrah unto Lasha.[9]

Down to Egypt

And he moved on from there to a mountain on the east of Bethel and pitched his tent with Bethel on the west and Ai on the east: and there he built an altar unto the Lord and called upon the name of the Lord.[10] Abram built [11]altars, which signified a place of worship and memorial to his spiritual encounter. The altar was a raised place not dissimilar to a table. It had four elevated corners called the horns. Incidentally Bethel was known as Luz in Abram's time thus we see the account is written by someone at a later time because Abram's grandson Jacob named the place Bethel. Ai was later burned to the ground by Joshua's armies. No trace has been found of Ai until this day.

Already Abram's new God had declared things that were incredible and went beyond the vision and dreams of ordinary men and women. So fantastic were the promises that one could barely comprehend and grasp the eternal issues presented because they passed human knowledge. Thus this God introduced

---

[8] They are listed as follows: Canaan begat Sidon his firstborn, followed by Heth, then the Jebusite, and the Amorite, and the Girgashite, and the Hivite, and the Arkite, and the Sinite, and the Arvadite, and the Zemarite, and the Hamathite.

[9] Genesis 10:15-19.

[10] Genesis 12:8

[11] The Hebrew word is mezbah, from zavach - to sacrifice. The Greek is omos, from baino - to come near or approach; The word is used with hieros, holy, and thusasterion, from thuo, to sacrifice.

Abram to a world of breath-taking wonder and awe. He imparted inspiration so staggering it seemed too difficult for the human mind to comprehend yet it was joyful to receive and a new sense of the meaning of Almighty began to dawn on Abram as never before. God proclaimed that Abram would receive the whole land of Canaan; Abram did not personally see that promise fulfilled nevertheless it did happen. God declared Abram would be the father of many nations: it also came to pass.

And Abram journeyed on still toward the south. And there was a famine in the land so he went down into Egypt to stay there for the famine was severe in the land. [12] A frequent famine pattern occurs through the Bible records and Abram reacts like any normal person would, he decides to go where the food is. We know why Abram went down into Egypt, but it is notable that God did not tell him to go there. Curiously before entering Egypt he said to Sarai his wife, "I know you are a fair woman to look upon so when the Egyptians see you they shall say, this is his wife and they will kill me, but they will save you alive. Tell them you are my sister and my soul shall live because of you.[13]"

Abram planned ahead for any unseen trouble. His strategy seemed based on two issues: his fear and the beauty of his wife. And sure enough Sarai's beauty captivated the Egyptians and the authorities took her to enhance the Pharaoh's harem. The Pharaoh seemed a reasonable man; he wanted to pay Abram a handsome dowry for his exotic Chaldean sister. Nonetheless this is a shocking situation for Abram, his wife is about to be married off to the king of Egypt. In

---

[12] Genesis 12: 9-10
[13] Genesis 12:11-13

those times the Pharaoh got first choice of all the beautiful women in the land. The Pharaoh appeared delighted with Sarai, he did not know that she was sixty-five years of age, but that was irrelevant, both young and mature women gave status to the Pharaoh's manhood.

Sarai through no choice of her own ended up in the king's harem. Moreover what would have followed when Pharaoh discovered his bride failed the virgin test? In addition the situation would be appalling for both Abram and Sarai if the Pharaoh defiled her. In fairness the Pharaoh trusted the report that she was Abram's sister, but the convention of forcibly taking a woman for the Pharaoh remained an unethical practice akin to kidnapping or hostage taking. Abram obviously feared for his life and suffered anxiety for Sarai. Simply the situation appeared too big for him, he had wealth but he did not possess the political power that the Pharaoh had.

Thus God plagued Pharaoh and his house with great plagues because of Sarai Abram's wife. [14] And Pharaoh called Abram and said, "What is this that you have done to me? Why did you say she is your sister and not your wife, I could have easily slept with her," he lamented with an angry voice. The Egyptians recognized the repercussions of injustice and adultery and they genuinely feared curses. All of Pharaoh's nightmares came upon him at once and he felt justifiably angry with Abram and commanded him to take his wife and get out of his sight.

---

[14] Genesis 12:17.

So Abram packed up and left Egypt with his wife and Lot, Sarai's brother, with all their possessions and travelled back to the south of Palestine. And Abram owned great riches in cattle, silver and gold. And he went on his journeys from the south to Bethel to the place where his tent had been at the beginning and the altar, which he constructed there at the beginning and he worshipped and called on the name of the Lord. And Lot also had flocks and herds and tents. [15]

Egypt had been a strange and degrading experience for the Chaldean couple yet it did expose some unique and fragile human traits. But how wonderful for Abram that God turned things for his benefit, the Pharaoh let Abram keep the dowry he paid for Sarai. Maybe he felt guilty about the bad ethics involved and his own selfish motives that got him into big trouble with the angry God of the Chaldean migrant. Perhaps he let Abram keep it to compensate for personal injury and humiliation caused to both Abram and Sarai; whatever the case he still deported them from Egypt to save face.

---

[15] Genesis 13:1-5.

Abram and Lot separate

Lot like uncle Abram had become a wealthy farmer. There comes a time in people's lives where they expand to such a degree that the place they inhabit can no longer sustain them. This is often a tricky period because wrong decisions can be made. Strife can sometimes be an indication of growth, it can also be ruinous.

Eventually the herdsmen of Abram's cattle and the herdsmen of Lot's cattle quarreled and got into strife with each other: and the Canaanite and the Perizzite dwelled then in the land.[16] And Abram said to Lot, "We are family let's not have strife between my herdsmen and your herdsmen it might spill over to you and me."

Abram appears as a gracious person. He makes for an interesting character study: he is kindly, hospitable, generous and courageous and has strong convictions. He is definitely a spiritual man but that does not mean he is free from making mistakes or bad decisions, however he certainly endeavors to honor his God.

True to his character he offered Lot the first option of choosing the east or west for grazing land. Lot chose the east, the plain of Jordan, a paradise at that time with Sodom situated nearby. Lot chose the apparent best option. He should have declined and deferred to his uncle Abram's seniority. Maybe Lot had things on his mind at that time. Sometimes people have to learn courteous quality traits as they do not come naturally. Lot made a serious mistake that created enormous consequences when he finally sold up and moved into

---

[16] Genesis 13:7

Sodom that extremely perverse and prosperous city. When strife causes us to separate from our established family and friends we need to weigh our decision carefully. Abraham in reality was a tower of strength to Lot, but at a crucial decision making moment Lot seemed ignorant of it.

Lot in Sodom

So Lot pitched his tent toward Sodom, which is the pathway to backsliding. Incidentally the men of Sodom were wicked and sinners before the Lord exceedingly.[17] Alas, Lot looked at Sodom next thing he became a citizen of Sodom. His flocks and herds were no longer necessary he no longer desired to be a tent dweller or herdsman anymore; the time had come for a different lifestyle and an opportunity to establish permanent roots for the family. Perhaps he still pined for the facilities of the great metropolis Ur.

And the Lord said unto Abram after Lot separated from him, "Lift up now your eyes and look from the place where you are northward and southward, and eastward and westward. All the land which you see, to you will I give it and to your seed forever. And I will make your seed as the dust of the earth so that if a man can number the dust of the earth then so shall your seed shall also be numbered. Arise and walk through the land in the length of it and in the breadth of it for I will give it unto you."

Then Abram dismantled his tent and came and camped in the plain of Mamre, which is in Hebron and

---

[17] Genesis 13:12-13

he built there an altar unto the Lord.[18] Despite the fact that Abram's numbers had decreased numerically due to Lot's withdrawal, God promised Abram seed innumerable. On that basis he needed to get up and move forward and experience the land. God's promises contradicted what the natural circumstances indicated. People should not always live for something to happen in the future, hope we need, but we need to choose a positive attitude now.

And it came to pass in the days of Amraphel king of Shinar, Arioch king of Ellasar, Chedorlaomer king of Elam, and Tidal king of nations; that these made war with Bera king of Sodom, and with Birsha king of Gomorrah, Shinab king of Admah, and Shemeber king of Zeboiim, and the king of Bela, which is Zoar.[19]

Modern historians have tried to identify these kings but they are not conclusive. Arioch has been proposed as Eri-Aku or Warad Larsa king of Larsa – 1830 BC. Amraphel has been named Hammurabi of Babylon. Tidal has been identified as Tudhaliya from Anatolia, but the dates appear too late to correspond with the kings mentioned. Josephus simply calls these kings Assyrians, which identifies their area of origin. The Canaanites paid tribute to the Northern kings for the past twelve years, but they rebelled in the thirteenth year. The result of their attempt for freedom was a punitive sweep by these northern armies taking in the country of the [20]Amalekites, which borders the Negev

---

[18] Genesis 13:14-18
[19] Genesis 14:1-2
[20] In Numbers 24:20 Amalek is called first among the nations. It seems to indicate to me that they were an early tribe living prior to Esau's grandson Amalek who is perceived to be the patriarch of the Amalekites - Gen 36:16. Immanuel Velikovsky who wrote the book: Chaos of the ages: makes the assertion that the Amalekites are none other than the Hyksos who dominated Egypt for some two hundred years. He claims that after they were defeated by Joshua at the valley of Rephidim, they went on to find Egypt in a devastated

to Shur near Egypt. Unfortunately Lot was captured and taken away by the Chaldeans. But fortuitously an escapee came directly to Abram or it would have been miserable slavery for Lot. Why did the escapee seek out Abram? Abram carried great respect in that country and had cordial relations with the Amorites in his vicinity: Mamre, Aner and Eschol who were privileged to have the Abram's friendship thus their names despite being Canaanites were recorded in scripture. The plain of Mamre near Hebron called Kiriath-Arba receives frequent mention in relation to Abram.

Abram assumed the role of a powerful leader supported by a considerable community. When the dreadful news arrived he rose to the occasion and galvanized his community to pursue the Chaldean captors, demonstrating great courage and self-sacrificing friendship. By means of a surprise attack, he successfully rescued Lot and many other captives along with the stolen loot from Sodom. Abram did not have the numbers militarily, but God was present with him. Abram's rescue of Lot foreshadows an ominous picture because in the near future angels will have to rescue Lot from another very dangerous and ugly circumstance.

And the king of Sodom went out to meet him after his return from the slaughter of Chedorlaomer and of the kings that were with him at the valley of Shaveh, which is the king's dale. And Melchizedek king of Salem brought forth bread and wine. He was the priest of the highest God, and he blessed Abram and said,

---

state and simply took over. It is a very interesting hypothesis. Veliovsky is considered radical in his thinking by some scholars.

"Blessed be Abram of the highest God, possessor of heaven and earth: and blessed be the highest God, which hath delivered your enemies into your hand. And Abram gave him tithes of all.[21]"

Melchizedek

Who was this mysterious king-priest? Nobody knows. We are introduced to him when he meets Abram after his stunning victory over the armies of Chedorlaomer. Also about to greet Abram was the King of Sodom. By a timely intervention however Melchizedek caused Abram to rest and be refreshed with a symbolic meal of bread and wine. This became a spiritual experience for Abram reminding him of God's protection, providence and future blessings. This is an unusual scene, Abram after a great victory is encompassed on one hand by the High Priest of God and on the other by the king of Sodom. An encounter of light and darkness: what moral can be extracted from this spectacle? Which party will influence Abram at a time of great success? Will it be light or darkness? One of the purposes of the Lord's Table is to strengthen believers to resist this world's substance.

Abram gave Melchizedek a tithe of all the spoils. The principle of tithing comes to us in Genesis and notably the Melchizedek priesthood existed before the priesthood of Levi and Aaron. This is also the first mention of the city of Jerusalem or yebu-salem (Salem-peace) in the Bible. King Melchizedek was the apparent founder in the forty-sixth year of Abram some two thousand years before the siege of

---

[21] Genesis 14:17-20

Vespasian and Titus. Salem meaning peace is a natural venue for the residence of the King Melchizedek, which means righteousness; his name also appears prophetically significant. When Joshua later conquered the Promised Land, the Jewish Tribe razed this Canaanite city with fire - Judges 1:8. Later we learn the Jebusites regained their hold on Jerusalem and did so for hundreds of years until king David's era - Judges 1:21.

Divine Rewards for Abram

After these things happened the word of the Lord came to Abram in a vision saying, "Fear not Abram, I am your shield and your exceeding great reward. [22]" Abram had declined fabulous riches after his defeat of the northern armies and the reason for his rejection seems that the spoils of battle were tainted by Sodom. Abram lived his life in Canaan guided by spiritual values that included [23] kosher and the virtues of self-control over covetousness, which is an enemy inside of the soul. Abram's Canaanite friends Mamre, Aner and Eschol, could not believe their ears when they overheard Abram tell the King of Sodom that he would not receive any rewards from Sodom. However he released his Canaanite friends to take whatever they wanted, which means they received a double portion at his expense. Abram's reward was the joy of knowing Lot had been saved, but in case of any doubt God spoke to him and said: "I am your exceeding great

---

[22] Genesis 15:1

[23] Kosher is a Yiddish word from the Hebrew kasher, meaning, lawful or proper. It is similar to the Arabic, halal, food prepared according to Islamic law.

reward." Only a spiritual man can fully comprehend the vastness of God's providence and comfort. Abram's true wealth resided in his relationship with God.

Abram then asked the Lord who would be his heir to all of the rewards that the Lord would bestow on him, as it stood his steward Eliezer appeared the only person in sight likely to receive the inheritance of Abram. Then and there the Lord promised Abram a son of his own and he brought him abroad to get a clear vista of the night sky and he asked Abram to count the stars if it were at all possible, for so shall Abram's seed be counted, myriads upon myriads. What a promise! What a fantastic episode in the Genesis. Abram believed God and he trusted that it would indeed come to pass. When we have faith in God's word it is counted or credited to us as righteousness. God looks no more upon our unworthiness, but he sees the perfect righteousness of Christ in our stead.

Hagar and Ishmael

The circumstances connected to the birth of Ishmael are as follows: Sarai, Abram's wife could not produce children, but as was common in those times rich people owned slaves and she had an Egyptian handmaid named Hagar. And Sarai said to Abram, "Look the Lord has restrained me from bearing. I want you to impregnate my slave that I may obtain children by her."

Abram listened to her proposal and followed her advice.[24] Surprisingly despite God's promises to Abram, Sarai his wife remained barren. She grew despondent after her ten years of barrenness in Canaan and the years before that in Ur and Haran thus she decided the time had come to assist God's promises and so she directed the proceedings at a crucial time. She took Hagar and gave her to Abram to be his wife. [25]

Surrogate motherhood is nothing new; it has been around for thousands of years. Sarai's impatience engineered this brilliant scheme of requisitioning Hagar to fill the vacuum. Hagar was a slave, probably acquired when they were in Egypt. No doubt she possessed pretty features for Sarai would only want the best for Abram.

Slaves occupied a low rank in ancient days with virtually no rights. Possession of slaves meant life was tolerably easy for folk in those patriarchal ages, but the owner had to provide shelter and feed them. Slaves could be a heavy burden in financially hard pressed times. A slave exploited as a concubine could not

---

[24] Genesis 16:1-2
[25] Genesis 16:3

expect the same honor and treatment a freeborn wife would receive. Therefore Hagar had no say in the matter. It remained legitimate in Old Testament times for a slave owner to gratify himself with a slave because she became his possession and therefore an automatic concubine. For a slave to be elevated to concubine status brought with it new benefits; the delighted handmaid found herself in bed under her master and she conceived. When she knew that she had conceived, true to human nature, she grew haughty and looked down upon Sarai with contempt.[26]

Abram had submissively complied with Sarai's request, yet was that surprising? Hagar the youthful and exotic Egyptian girl had been thrust into his arms as a gift from his wife. Of course he enjoyed all Hagar had to offer and he probably felt revitalised. Sure enough she fell pregnant. But consider the disposition of the slave girl: when elevated and intimately enjoyed by her newly impassioned master she became haughty and insolent to her mistress; the slave disdained her sterile benefactor.

Sarai said unto Abram, "May you suffer for this wrong against me, I gave my maid to you and now that she is pregnant she despises me, well the Lord determine which of us is right." But Abram feeling bewildered said to Sarai, "Look she is your slave, it's up to you to sort her you. Do whatever you think is necessary." Sarai immediately dealt severely with her and Hagar fled from her face.[27]

It is never prudent to elevate a slave to the position of the master's wife it will not work. And in Old Testament terms: what fellowship does a Hebrew have

---

[26] Genesis 16:4
[27] Genesis 16:5-6

with an Egyptian? Unbelief has unbelievable fertility. Hagar felt elevated above Sarai and she despised her as a barren subordinate. Sarai, who will not tolerate any of this nonsense realizes her mistake and proceeds to blame Abram for the ugly situation. Abram never blamed anybody for his mistakes, he remained calm in personality. Surrogate motherhood enjoyed wide acceptance in those times but it created serious problems. However the furious Sarai exercised her authority with Abram's full consent and how discouraging for young Hagar, her newfound bliss quickly turned sour. If only she had been thankful and had more wisdom and maturity then life would have been more genteel and relaxed.

Sarai turned into an oppressive tyrant who tormented Hagar and demonstrated some nasty Sumerian qualities, but justifiably so. Slaves need to learn courtesy and humility particularly when offered great honors. Not surprisingly the disillusioned and hurting Hagar fled for her life, (Hagar means flight) and she probably wondered how everything had turned sour. Maybe she even questioned how Abram permitted such cruel treatment to be inflicted upon her since she had now conceived and carried his very own child. But Hagar was a slave. Abram's status in life and his culture were well beyond her banal thinking. There had only ever been one woman in his life – Sarai, and she retained his love. No Egyptian maid could ever displace his Sumerian bride. It is not that he did not care, he probably felt bad for Hagar, but protocol and love compelled him to support Sarai.

And the angel of the Lord found Hagar by a fountain of water in the wilderness on the way to Shur. And he said, "Hagar, Sarai's maid, what are you doing and where will you go?" And she said, "I flee from the face of my mistress Sarai." And the angel of the Lord said unto her: "Return to your mistress, and submit yourself under her hands. "[28]

The Lord found her in a distressed state by the fountain of Shur in the wilderness. Shur was not far from the Egyptian border; Hagar obviously tried to find her way home to Egypt. The angel instructed her to remember her position and return to the safety of the tent of Abram and he gave a wonderful promise concerning her child to help restore her discouraged spirit. The angel also prophesied about the nature of this child. "I will multiply your seed exceedingly that it shall not be numbered for multitude." And the angel of the Lord said unto her, "Look you are with child and shall bear a son and you shall call his name Ishmael because the Lord has heard your affliction. And he will be a wild man, his hand will be against every man, and every man's hand against him; and he shall dwell in the presence of all his brethren.[29]"

This covenant of Hagar is descriptive of Sinai that pictures the Law and bondage. Ishmael represents the natural man or carnal nature, which is wild, unruly, and dwells right in our midst creating perpetual discord with the spiritual nature - Romans 7:21-25. Hagar had met more than an angel; she had encountered the living God. She called him Beer-la-hai-roi – that is the One who lives and sees me.

What a touching description of the Lord who cares and knows the number of hairs on our head. The New Testament does not look favorably upon Hagar; she is typed as the Law of bondage - Galatians 4:30. There is

---

[28] Genesis 16:7-9
[29] Genesis 16:10-12

something sad about Hagar: first an object of pleasure, then a victim of scorn and a vent for anger and frustration from Sarai. One moment she enjoys the comfort of Abram's bedroom next she is beaten and thrown out as a solo mother with nothing to her name but a disowned pregnancy. This young woman felt weak, burned by the sun, and in a state of distress and shock as she ran away from home. She probably felt unwanted; it seemed like a total rejection. With nowhere to go and no one to turn to, life can suddenly turn sour. Yet the Lord saw the aimless wandering of the pregnant slave girl and her soreness of body caused by Sarai's beating, and he saw her broken spirit caused by Abram's rejection. Life can be hard but God watched over her, making sure she came to no harm.

It was not a matter of rights or wrongs; she had neither rights nor claims. She had been given a privilege, but pride had caused her downfall. She tried to play a power game, but she found herself out of her league, and she ran away from the problem. Right or wrong God finds us regardless of failures, pride, humiliations and wrecked lives; he sees us and wants to help us find the way.

What was the angel's advice? "Go home and act as you should; remember your place and I will fulfil my promise to you." He does not justify our wrongs, instead he forgives us. Hagar's pregnancy was not ordained of God, but God rescued her, and he will help us out with our weaknesses of the flesh. So Hagar submitted to Sarai, and Abram obtained his firstborn son. This caused great joy for him at eighty-six years of age, naturally he doted over Ishmael.

Ishmael is the classic example of the permissive will of God; something that is a result of the will of the flesh. Abram never considered God when he took the Egyptian as a wife. It all appeared so natural and logical and the circumstances seemed right. But Abram listened to the voice of his wife rather than God's voice. It is easier to hear a woman than to hear God. By this stage Abram had been in the land for ten years however even though he experienced profound encounters with Yahweh Elohim yet he was still relatively inexperienced in maintaining total obedience to the revelation he had received. Maybe when Hagar conceived it seemed to him like a divine confirmation because everything fell into place so simply. Alas the things that fell into place soon crumbled and fell apart; Ishmael brought contention into the family.

The Abrahamic Covenant

Soon after that emotional domestic problem and despite both Sarai and Abram's error of Judgment God made a covenant with Abram who along with Sarai received a change of name to celebrate the amazing event – Genesis 17:5. The Covenant is one of faith and immense revelation from God concerning future history. The fulfilment of this Covenant was unconditional and dependent solely on God.

Here is a list of great promises found in Genesis:

1. "I will make you a great nation; I will bless you and make your name great; and you shall be a blessing" - 12:2.

2. "I will bless those who bless you and I will curse him who curses you; and in you all the families of the earth shall be blessed" - 12:3.

3. "To your descendants I will give this land" - 12:7.

4. "And I will make your descendants as the dust of the earth so that if a man could number the dust of the earth then your descendants also could be numbered." - 13:16.

5. Then He brought him outside and said, "Look now toward heaven, and count the stars if you are able to number them." And He said to him, "So shall your descendants be" - 15:5.

6. And he believed in the Lord and He accounted it to him for righteousness - 15:6.

7. "My covenant is with you and you shall be a father of many nations" - 17:4.

8. "I will make you exceedingly fruitful; and I will make nations of you and kings shall come from you" - 17:6.

9. "In Isaac your seed shall be called" - 21:12.

10. "Your descendants shall possess the gate of their enemies" - 22:17.

For Noah, the rainbow appeared as a sign of the Covenant. But for [30]Abraham, male circumcision on the eighth day became the sign of the Covenant. [31] Circumcision was the sole stipulation in this contract, but note that it came after God had already chosen Abraham - Romans 4:9-13.

The signs of the Covenants represent God's signature on his contracts. The rainbow like starry nights is a beautiful signature of God visibly manifest for all

---

[30] Genesis 17:5 - Abraham, Father or ancestor of many nations. Genesis 17:15 - Sarah means princess.
[31] Genesis 17:10-14.

mankind; though in reality all of creation remains his abiding signature.

For Abraham's Covenant circumcision seems a rather dramatic and unique sign. Because it is a Covenant that calls for faith it requires human co-operation and involves pain. Interestingly enough the Abrahamic Covenant did not negate the Noahic Covenant, it revealed more specifically God's plan of redemption. Noah's Covenant remains a token of God' promise that the earth will never be destroyed again by a flood whereas Abraham's Covenant was specifically for Abraham and his descendants through Isaac, but culminating eventually for all humanity through the promised seed of Abraham who would be the Messiah.

How does the Abrahamic Covenant affect Christians? It affects believers only in the great truths that we learn from it: through Jesus the Messiah we have seen the complete fulfilment of God's promises to Abraham. Indeed Christians are now the spiritual descendants of Abraham through the same faith that he exercised in God - That he might be the father of all who believe, though they be not circumcised; that righteousness might be imputed unto them also - Romans 4:11.

One can only enter into the New Covenant by faith: that is by exercising trust the same way that Abraham believed. For God rewards the act of faith by imparting to the believer his own righteousness like he did with Abraham; it is in that sense that Abraham becomes the father of faith. However Christians are not obliged to be circumcised because circumcision is an inner spiritual matter that ratifies the New Covenant. Obviously cutting the flesh is a physical issue that cannot renew the spirit of a man. Paul said in the New Testament that circumcision is nothing and uncircumcision is nothing, but the keeping of the commandments of God is the important thing - 1Corinthians 7:19.

Stating the obvious, circumcision is a sensitive subject. Why God chose it as a sign of his covenant with Abraham is both remarkable and awkward. It is generally not spoken about freely from the pulpit simply because of the intimate nature of the subject. Paul said that less honorable parts of the body get greater honor and the intimate parts have greater modesty – 1Corinthians 12:23. There are manifold scriptures relating to circumcision because it became compulsory for the Israelites under the Law of Moses. The chosen people of God were identifiable by circumcision. But how does one know that a person is circumcised because generally people are clothed? But God knows who is and who is not.

In the New Testament circumcision is used as a figure of speech for the spiritual heart, and likewise, one cannot see the physical heart of men because they are clothed with a body. Circumcision itself entails cutting away the foreskin from the penis. It is considered by some to be a mutilation and unnecessary. That seems true because Adam appears to have been created with foreskin.

For the male, in terms of scriptural symbolism, the removal of the foreskin exposes the sensitive glans of the penis. The spiritual application reveals that a circumcision of the heart removes the foreskin or skin that has deadened the sensitivity of the heart to spiritual values and awareness. Spirituality and worship is an intimate experience and the Song of Solomon is viewed in that context. An intimate experience with a lover ideally involves sexual expression that is life producing. The male member is potentially a life giving fountain and therefore an honorable and important body-part. Clinically speaking, the exposed male glans is more sensitive to sensation than one covered with foreskin. There is also the sanitary issue involved: the foreskin traps bacteria that can cause infection. Taking all this into consideration, the covenant of circumcision is pregnant, for want of a better word, with meaning. The actual operation or cutting is painful and this itself carries significant spiritual meaning. To suggest that there is no pain involved in a spiritual experience is not valid. The cutting of skin on an acutely sensitive part of the body is enough to make most people squeamish. The same goes for the spiritual heart. There is intense pain involved in the spiritual circumcision of the heart.

Visitation

One afternoon, Abraham enjoyed a leisurely siesta when he suddenly saw three significant men approaching him, which made him run and bow before them. Aware these strangers were not ordinary men he began to solicit their company with the usual hospitality niceties customary in those times. Abraham knew his God; he could identify him whenever they physically met. He hastened into the tent to Sarah and said, "Quickly make three servings of fine meal and cook cakes upon the hearth." Abraham ran to the herd and fetched a calf, tender and good, and gave it to a young man who hurried to prepare it. He took butter and milk and the calf, which he had dressed, and when cooked he set it before the men and he stood by them under the tree as they partook of the served food. [32]

Here is a curious thing: practicing Jews do not serve dairy products like butter, milk and cheese when eating beef. Abraham however served butter, bread, milk and beef to the Lord God.

There are a number of appearances in the scriptures of God in human form, they are referred to as a theophany or a visible appearance of God in human form; Hindus use the word avatar and scholarly critics use the term anthropomorphisms. This special home visit happened because God came to announce that [33]Sarah would shortly fall pregnant. It is interesting to note the three men spoke as one person. I always assumed the other two men were ordinary angels because of the two angels who went into Sodom to rescue Lot. But I need to rethink this story because the term 'angel of the Lord' is also used in Old Testament language for an appearance of God in human form and I can see a Trinity picture here. "Where is Sarah your wife?" The man asked. "She is in the tent," he replied. "I will return to you this time next year and Sarah your wife shall have a son."

And Sarah heard what he said from behind the tent door. "How can we enjoy sex now that we are old?" she [34] mused and laughed to herself. Sarah and Abraham were obviously past their amorous years. Sarah had experienced the menopause; quite literally she could not have children because she no longer ovulated. The dramatic news amused her, and she

---

[32] Genesis 18:6-8

[33] Sarah means princess: possibly an expansion of the name Sarai, meaning, my princess, to that of Sarah, a princess in a sovereign realm.

[34] Genesis 18:9-12

laughed quietly, contemplating the unlikely possibility of sexual pleasure.

The Hebrew word for pleasure derives from Eden as in the Garden of Eden. Whether Sarah had fully understood who she entertained is not clear however the stranger's statement startled her. The Lord said to Abraham, "Why did Sarah laugh saying, surely I am too old to bear a child? Is anything too hard for the Lord? At the time appointed I will return unto you according to the time of life and Sarah shall have a son. [35]" God heard every word Sarah thought in her heart, and he challenged her because he knew she listened in from behind the tent skin.

The whole meaning of Abraham's life and destiny involved the child of promise and that child must be the result of a divine miracle. He must stand in absolute contrast to any machinations of the flesh such as the conception of Ishmael which Sarah proposed. The miracle son who symbolizes the Christ must not come from the desire or [36]impulse of man, but entirely because of the plans, purposes and direct intervention of God Almighty.

There are fantastic principles inherent in the statement 'at the time appointed.' First, nothing is impossible for God, and second, there is an appointed time for his miracles to come to pass, meaning faith is tested and patience is learned. Then Sarah denied it saying, "I didn't laugh." She immediately felt nervous. And the angel said, "[37] Nay; but you did laugh[38]." Sarah

---

[35] Genesis 18:13-14

[36] John 1:12-13 But as many as received him, to them he gave power to become the sons of God, even to them that believe on his name , which were born, not of blood, nor of the will of the flesh, nor of the will of man, but of God.

[37] Nay- adverb: used to introduce a second and stronger expression in a sentence when the first expression is not sufficient.

[38] Genesis 18:15

realizes who it is she is dealing with and feels overcome with a sense of awe and fear.

What are the results of fear? Remember Adam and Eve? When they felt fear they hid. How did Sarah react? She denied her thoughts of unbelief and her sudden fear placed her in a state of denial. How did God respond to her denial? He gently chided her because he understood her personality and the situation. Sarah generally had no need to lie, but on this occasion, fear overcame her and she reacted accordingly; nevertheless, she chose an inappropriate moment to doubt the power of the living God.

Lot and his daughters

Abraham knew that something terrible was coming and he eventually witnessed the dreadful smoke rising in the air like a furnace. The plains of Mamre in the Judean hills lie above the Jordan Valley and Dead Sea region and the cities of the Plain were not a considerable distance for a visual sighting of smoke plumes rising up out of the valley.

And it came to pass when God destroyed the cities of the plain that God remembered Abraham and sent Lot out of the midst of the overthrow when he destroyed the cities in which Lot dwelt. And Lot went up out of Zoar with his two daughters and dwelt in the mountain for he feared to dwell in Zoar, and he dwelt in a cave he and his two daughters.[39]

---

[39] Genesis 19: 29-30

Brimstone and fire hit the cities of the Plain with a colossal and paralyzing blast. Lot almost suffered cardiac arrest, and only then did the dreadfulness of the situation dawn on him. It became a frightening morning for the city of Zoar, the inhabitants felt the flames almost reach out and lick their city. Every heart stood still at the devastating catastrophe. In scenarios like this, people have literally suffered seizures, hair has turned white, and many people lose control of their bowels for lesser incidents. Lot and his daughters had sought refuge in Zoar, and as they fled, Lot's wife ignored the patent warning of the angels and she looked back and sealed her own fate by turning into a pillar of salt. Lot had left other family members to die in Sodom, and then in a moment of typical human folly, his foolish wife was snatched from him in judgment.

When the scorching blare of Sodom blistered the environment his feebleness and indecision, which manifested the night before when the angels warned him to get out of Sodom, quickly disappeared. But Lot actually restrained judgment from falling on the city because the longer he lingered the more he delayed the fire falling upon the cities. Incredibly Lot even fell into haggling with the angel.

And it came to pass when the angel escorted Lot and family outside of the city that he said, "Escape for your life, look not behind you neither stay in all the plain, escape to the mountain so you will not be consumed." And Lot said unto them, "Oh not so my Lord. Look now your servant has found grace in your sight and you have magnified your mercy which you have shown to me in saving my life. I cannot escape to the mountain lest some evil take me and kills me.

Behold now this city is near to flee to and it is a little one. Oh, let me escape to it, see it's only a little one? And my soul shall live." And the Angel said unto him, "Look I have accepted you concerning this thing also that I will not overthrow this city for which you have spoken. Make haste and escape there for I cannot do anything till you are there." Therefore the name of the city was called Zoar.[40]

The angel, restrained by Lot, acknowledged that he was unable to carry out his mission until Lot reached a place of safety away from the judgment. The graciousness of God towards Lot, and for that fact, any of his chosen, is one of great care and security against harm and judgment. Lot got in the way of God's purpose. Finally, with a trembling heart he escaped to the mountains where he should have gone in the first place. After the magnitude of the traumatizing incendiary that engulfed the cities, a very nervous and shocked Lot felt insecure and unsafe anywhere on the Plain.

I ponder Zoar's escape because it figured on the termination schedule. Strangely and unwittingly, Lot saved Zoar, and the odd thing is the inhabitants of Zoar were immune and unaware that he secured their lives; and the way he secured it was bizarre. Sure, he should never have fled there, yet it was a divine commission in the sense that he saved the city. The Angel consented to remove Zoar off the termination list because Lot appeared disoriented and complaining. The city did not survive, not because of the fire, it escaped that, but because the eco-system of the Plain

---

[40] Genesis 19:17-22

remained forever altered and became unfavorable to habitation.

Why God had second thoughts about Bela, also known as Zoar, remains open to speculation, but her escape was a miraculous demonstration of grace in so many different aspects for grace alone saved Zoar.

The mountains, nearest the Vale of Siddim where he fled are none other than the mountains of Moab. Today it is the country of Jordan, but before the Moabites the Emim, a sub-tribe of the Rephaim Canaanites, abode there.

Once in the mountains the escapees had to come to terms with their situation and rehabilitation. That required time and re-invention, but the holocaust had disoriented the daughters of Lot. They thought the whole earth had suffered judgment; why they reasoned that is too complex to determine. Nonetheless, their state of mind motivated them to commit incest with their father. They did not behave out of a depraved mind rather they acted hastily without giving themselves time to prove whether the judgment was local or universal.

I can't imagine where they got the wine from to make their father drunk. Perhaps the angels had made sure they took provisions with them. Lot in his drunken condition, did not know that he was the victim of a conspiracy; he neither consented nor encouraged what took place. His heart must have sunk within him when he discovered that his daughters carried his children. The daughters remained influenced by the rationality of Sodom.

Eventually, the oldest daughter gave birth to a son and called his name Moab: the same is the father of the Moabites unto this day. And the younger also gave birth to a son and she called his name Ben-ammi: he is the father of the children of Ammon unto this day.[41] The nations of Moab and Ammon appear frequently in the scriptures. A notable character to come from Moab was the lovely Ruth. The capital of the modern Kingdom of Jordan is Amman, which is testimony to the ancient descendants of Lot.

Lot genuinely believed the Lord God, and God remembered him and counted him as righteous, but he lived in an appalling carnal city. His life remains a memorial set up by God to warn of the folly of trying to live for both worlds. Jesus draws our attention to the seriousness of that error: "Remember Lot's wife" - Luke 17:32.

Abimelech and the Philistines

And Abraham journeyed toward the south country, and dwelled between Kadesh and Shur and sojourned in Gerar. And Abraham said of Sarah his wife, "She is my sister." And Abimelech king of Gerar took Sarah with the intention of putting her into his harem. [42] Abraham's walk through the land brought him into Philistine country, which encompassed the coast mentioned. The locality is identified as the general area of Gaza. We learn in the genealogies that the Philistines were from the line of Ham through Mizraim's son Casluhim and that they emerged from the land of Capthorim - Genesis 10:14; Jeremiah 47:4 & Amos

---

[41] Genesis 19:37-38
[42] Genesis 20: 1-2

9:7. Capthtor is supposedly the Island of Crete, but it cannot be verified. Philistine pottery and other archaeological finds are chiefly of Mycenaean derivation.

There is a sense of déjà-vu in this story because when Abraham entered the Philistine areas he appears not to have learned any lessons from his Egyptian sojourn; once again he felt vulnerable and feared for his life because of his beautiful wife. Though somewhat aged, Sarah yet retained her youthful beauty, so when Abraham moved into the principality of Gerar, the same customs applied as in Egypt - the king had first option on women. Under normal circumstances this situation would have been an honor for any family as it gave an alliance with the royalty of the land. However, this was not a normal situation. When the Philistines forcibly detained Sarah and brought her to the King's harem, God appeared to him in a dream and said, "You are a dead man Abimelech." Abraham by his actions had literally set the Pharaoh and Abimelech in opposition to God. When Abimelech pleaded his innocence, God indicated that he had prevented Abimelech from sinning and knew that Abraham's lie had instigated the predicament. Nevertheless, if Abimelech did not release Sarah he would surely die. Abimelech got the message loud and clear.

Kings ruled supreme in ancient times and were corrupted by their power that corrupted them with pride and haughtiness. But Abimelech, in shock, took the message of God seriously. It is easy to sympathize with the Philistine King because he had valid reason to be upset with Abraham, but once again, the prerogative of the King's supposedly divine right for first choice to the women in the land caused problems.

Abraham's fear had caused the situation; it resembled the same fear that he felt in Egypt. When Abraham's fragile weaknesses were tested, he succumbed to carnality and was unable to remain on a high spiritual plain. Without divine intervention, he would have lost Sarah. Abraham had a long-standing agreement with Sarah: when they entered foreign lands she had to acknowledge that he was her brother.

After his nightmare meeting with God, Abimelech took sheep and oxen and men servants and women servants and gave them unto Abraham as a settlement for his distress and humiliation, and restored to him Sarah his wife. And Abimelech said, "Behold, my land is before you: dwell where it pleases you. And to Sarah he said, Observe, I have given your brother a thousand pieces of silver."[43]

The Philistine king had had a close encounter and wanted to repair the damage done and establish goodwill between himself and Abraham and so remove the curse afflicting the Philistine women. In contrast, the Pharaoh told Abram to get out of his sight, but Abimelech happily gave Abraham visiting rights. Abimelech took the opportunity to reprove Sarah for she went along with the duplicity and thus endangered her chastity to Abraham. As it turned out, because of God, Abraham prospered even in a time of failure. So Abraham prayed to God and God healed Abimelech and his wife and his maidservants and they produced children for the Lord had fast closed up all the wombs of the house of Abimelech because of Sarah, Abraham's wife.[44] This is the first recorded physical

---

[43] Genesis 20:14-16
[44] Genesis 20:17-18

healing in answer to prayer. Abraham had previously interceded for the life of Lot and his family, and thus we saw the gracious disposition of God who said if there were ten righteous people in Sodom and Gomorrah he would not destroy those cities. Shortly after that, Abraham looked toward Sodom and Gomorrah and the smoke of the country went up as the smoke of a furnace. It was directly after this dramatic horror that Abraham sojourned in Gerar where the old problem of fear manifested itself. And Sarah also subjected herself to his fear; one can have a visitation from God and yet fail due to human fears.

Isaac and Ishmael

And the Lord visited Sarah as he had said, and the Lord did unto Sarah as he had spoken. For Sarah conceived, and bore Abraham a son in his old age, at the set time of which God had spoken to him. [45] God had rejuvenated both Sarah and Abraham, nature was set in reverse, and it was a wondrous miracle. At last the promise had been fulfilled, Abraham waited and had not staggered at the promise of God with doubt or unbelief, even though circumstances seemed to defy what God had said would come to pass. For the natural mind it looked impossible for God's promise to come true, but Abraham's faith remained unquenchable and rock solid.

And Abraham called the name of his son that was born unto him whom Sarah bare to him, Isaac. [46] Isaac means laughter. Abraham had found the promise

---

[45] Genesis 21:1-2
[46] Genesis 21:3

amusing – Genesis 17:17 And Sarah had laughed in disbelief – Genesis 18:15. God had the last laugh, but God's laugh is shared around for others to enjoy the life that comes from him. And Abraham circumcised his son Isaac being eight days old, as God had commanded him. And Abraham reached the age of a hundred years when his son Isaac was born unto him. And Sarah said, "God hath made me to laugh, so that all that hear will laugh with me."[47]

What joy Sarah felt. For so long she had been the barren one, indeed she had passed the age of child bearing and all hope of bearing a child for Abraham had faded. Psychologically, people carry a self-induced guilt, torment and questions... 'I am different, I've failed, and why me?' One can be married to a wealthy man, have all life can offer, even great personal beauty, yet inside there is a gnawing misery that would trade all of the riches and personal beauty just to be able to have a baby and be normal. The instinct of motherhood is strong inside a woman. Sarah's stigma disappeared at ninety years of age; tears of joy celebrated the occasion.

So Abraham hosted a celebration party for the son of his old age, but during the celebrations Sarah spied Ishmael mocking the baby. Ishmael reacted like any normal adolescent, when the focus shifted from him onto a new baby, he found it difficult to handle and began manifesting irritation and mocked the child.

Ishmael represents the carnal or human nature whereas Isaac is the son of promise and therefore represents the spiritual aspect; even symbolizing Christ the son of promise. The human nature mocks

---

[47] Genesis 22:4-6

the heaven born nature and that is why Christians experience huge conflict in their souls and lives - Galatians 4:28.

The Jewish historian Josephus claims that Sarah originally treated Ishmael as her own child, which is probably true because Hagar was her slave and therefore Ishmael belonged to Sarah. Sarah potentially saw trouble looming for Isaac and she did not want Ishmael to usurp Isaac's inheritance, so she made a strategic move to cast out the slave woman and her offspring. It appears cruel, but eternal issues were at stake and Sarah got it right. It was ironical because the situation had been instigated by her in the first place; however when the crisis emerged she protected the Birthright inheritance of her free born son and unwittingly carried out the work of God. We also learn the spiritual principle that what takes place first in the natural realm, happens also in the spiritual dimension. Thus Ishmael, who mocks Isaac, is the natural, and he represents the fallen human nature, which persecutes those who are spiritual and have faith in God.

Although instinctive and easy for Sarah, Abraham experienced a genuine heart-breaking for he loved his child Ishmael. Before Isaac's birth, Abraham longed for Ishmael to be the special child of promise. Those emotions arose because he had not experienced Isaac at that time; Ishmael dominated his father-heart instincts. Abraham had set himself up for disappointment because God had already pre-determined that the child must go; Ishmael would obstruct the foreordained birth of the Christ. No man hates his own body or his own flesh and blood, but however grievous for Abraham his mistake must be cast out; nothing must oppose the second child, the

43

seed of faith. This is our lesson: the flesh must be cast off, the child of the bondwoman must be cast out, and there can be no mercy shown; in Christian terms it is called - dying to the flesh. The old life and nature must be cast out when God's gift of grace comes into the Believer's heart. Isaac and Ishmael cannot live and fellowship together for they are at enmity one with the other.

And God said unto Abraham, "Let it not be a grievous thing in your sight because of the lad, and because of your bondwoman; in all that Sarah has said to you, hear her voice; for it is through Isaac that your seed be named.[48]" Here is a specific covenant: in Isaac shall your seed be called. It is not 'in all' of Abraham's physical descendants that the covenant applies to, but only 'in Isaac's seed.' That is singular. Who is the ultimate seed or offspring from Isaac? It is Christ.

And as for Ishmael the son of the bondwoman, I will make him to become a nation because he is your seed. So Abraham rose up early in the morning, and took bread, and a skin-bottle of water, and gave it unto Hagar, putting it on her shoulder, and along with her child he sent her away: and she departed, and wandered in the wilderness of Beersheba.[49] Abraham must have felt a vacillating and wished he had never indulged in his carnal decision, but it was imperative for him to obey God in this matter.

It seemed merciless to cast out Hagar with her thirteen-year-old son. Why did not Abraham provide her with sufficient or a little extra to see her through? He was under strict instructions from God and Sarah to cast her out. These things were written for our benefit

---

[48] Genesis 21:12
[49] Genesis 21:13-14

and caution; Abraham did not understand it at all. Eventually, the water was spent in the bottle, and she pushed her son under one of the bushes. She went and sat about a bowshot away: for she said, "Let me not see the death of the child. And as she watched him she lifted her voice and wept." [50]

Hagar found herself cast adrift in the world with only a little water and bread. When these were used up the child weakened and finally with great emotion swelling up inside her being she prepared for his death. And God heard the voice of the lad; and the angel of God called to Hagar out of heaven, and said unto her, "What ails you, Hagar? Fear not, for God has heard the voice of the lad where he is. Arise, lift up the lad, and hold him in your hand, for I will make him a great nation." And God opened her eyes, and she saw a well of water; and she went, and filled the bottle with water and gave the lad drink. [51]

In the Bible, many wonderful incidents take place around a well; the wells seem to appear out of the desert. That is what God is able to do, make fountains appear in dry places - Isaiah 43:19-20. And God was with the lad; and he grew, and dwelt in the wilderness, and became an archer. And he dwelt in the wilderness of Paran: and his mother took him a wife out of the land of Egypt. Paran is the wilderness area that stretches from the Gulf of Aqaba westward to Shur. It is a semi fertile wilderness and ideal hunting ground for the early Arabian or Ishmaelite, as they were then known. The Arabian nations are the descendants of

---

[50] Genesis 21:15-16
[51] Genesis 21:17-19

Ishmael; Arabs therefore are an ethnic mixture of Hebrew and Egyptian.[52]

Beersheba

Abraham and his community had been dwelling around the Gerar area all this time. Relations with the Philistines had been cordial; because Abraham seemed a wealthy chief with a large community around him the Philistine king naturally wanted to make a treaty with him. He could foresee Abraham's posterity grow stronger and become a force to be reckoned with. Abimelech, and indeed Phichol, the chief captain, appear to be official titles: Abimelech means, my father king; a logical title for a royal position, and Phichol means, voice of the people. Phichol as captain represents the people. These titles were similar to titles such as Pharaoh or the later Caesar.

It is difficult to know if the kingdom of Gerar was the only Philistine settlement or whether the other four states, Gath, Ekron, Ashdod, and Ashkelon, were already in their embryonic stages. It is even possible that the eventual Pentapolis confederation of the Philistines evolved from this initial Philistine migration, which settled in Gerar, and after consolidation, proceeded to expand along the coastal region. Because the Philistines had coastal ports, they secured contact with the Mediterranean cultures that flourished and they retained their Mycenaean and Cretan links. This evolution did not happen immediately, just as the race of the Israelites took many hundreds of years to be

---

[52] Genesis 21:20-21

molded into a national ethnic group. Little is known of the Philistines and therefore much is speculation, but we do know that the Philistines were contemporary with Abraham and existed in [53] Palestine prior to the 12th Century BC.

And Abraham reproved Abimelech because of a well of water, which Abimelech's servants had violently taken away. Abimelech said, "I do not know who has done this thing neither did you tell me, neither yet have I heard about it until now."[54] Problems occur when in the midst of Philistines, indeed, they are prone to violence, yet many unbelievers possess good principles and virtue, as did Abimelech. Abraham's reproof led to a water rights agreement between the two parties. And Abraham took sheep and oxen and gave them to Abimelech; and both of them made a covenant. And Abraham set seven ewe lambs of the flock by themselves. And Abimelech said unto Abraham, "What does these seven ewe lambs mean which you have set by themselves?" And he said, "These seven ewe lambs are for you to take from my hand that they may be a witness unto me, that I have dug this well." Wherefore he called that place Beersheba because it was there they both made a vow. Thus, they made a covenant at Beersheba. Then Abimelech rose up, and Phichol the chief captain of his host, and they returned into the land of the Philistines.[55]

The familiar pattern is followed when the covenant is enjoined; in this case the seven ewes symbolize the oath that they made. Beersheba is the name of the

---

[53] Palestine is named after the Philistines.
[54] Genesis 21:25-26.
[55] Genesis 21:27-32

covenant, it means, 'the well of seven, or oath.' Oath therefore is from the Hebrew word seven, usually seven victims confirmed the oath or covenant; in this case, it was the seven ewes. Seven is a sacred number. Also, note that Abraham's servants dug the well. Water was an exceeding precious commodity; the Philistines violently took possession of the well. Abraham seems to have had greater expertise in tapping wells than the Philistines; and the Philistines when returning to their own country did not consider the Beersheba area as their country; probably they were happy to control the area only.

And Abraham planted a grove in Beersheba and there he called on the name of the Lord, the Everlasting God.[56] Abraham planted [57]Tamarisks. The trees were a reminder of God's goodness and protection of Abraham because he called upon the name of Yahweh El Olam, The Everlasting God. Abraham evidently enjoyed the Beersheba environment. It is a rolling grassland area, quite different to the more rugged hill country usually associated with Israel. The covenant entered into by Abraham with Abimelech covered three generations, but Isaac had problems with the Philistines later. The Israelites took possession of Beersheba in the wars of Joshua and he allotted it to the tribe of Simeon.

---

[56] Genesis 21:33

[57] Salt Cedar tree: deciduous.

Isaac sacrifice

And it came to pass after these things that God [58]tested Abraham and said unto him, "Abraham." And he said, "I am here Lord." And he said, "Take now your son, your only son Isaac, whom you love, and go to the land of Moriah and offer him there for a burnt offering upon one of the mountains which I will tell you of.""

The sacrifice of Isaac is another testing time for Abraham: that God asked for a human sacrifice appeared radical. This ordeal that stood before Abraham is pregnant with prophetic imagery, for in Isaac is the promise, and this story will preview what will happen to the ultimate promised Seed who is not yet evident. And God wanted to test whether Abraham remained true to his original vision and calling. Is Abraham devoted to God or has the focus shifted to his son whom God gave to Abraham? This is the nature of the test, but God uses this trial to reveal to Believers, the Messiah pre-Calvary and post-Calvary.

Abraham rose up early in the morning and saddled an ass and took two of his young men with him and Isaac his son and cut the wood for the burnt offering, and off he went to the place where God told him.[59] The wood preparation illustrates the cross; the two young men are witnesses of the account, and Abraham goes specifically to a place that God has told him to go. That place [60]Moriah is none other than the parcel of land, which became known as the threshing floor of [61]Ornan

---

[58] Hebrew- nacah נָסָה (naw-saw), to test.

[59] Genesis 22:3

[60] Hebrew- seen of Yahweh, or the place where Yahweh provides.

[61] 1 Chronicles 21:15-25

the Jebusite and later became the Temple site upon which stands the Mosque of Omar this day.

On the third day, Abraham lifted up his eyes and saw the place afar off. And Abraham said unto his young men, "Abide here with the ass; and I and the lad will go yonder and worship, and come again to you."[62] Abraham knew he was required to slay Isaac, but he felt sure God would intervene. It is hard to know if Abraham specifically foresaw Isaac's resurrection, but he assuredly spoke faith when he uttered the words, 'we will come again' to the witnesses. The three days mentioned also signifies the number three associated with Christ on the cross.

And Abraham took the wood of the burnt offering, and laid it upon Isaac his son and he took the fire in his hand, and a knife; and they went both of them together.[63] Laying the wood on the back of Isaac, the promised son, is the most explicit illustration of Jesus bearing the cross to Calvary. The fire and knife symbolized the suffering that awaits the Son of man; the fire as a burning and painful suffering; the knife as the instruments that would pierce his body. Genesis is thoroughly consistent in its theme of the redemptive work that God planned to achieve.

And Isaac spoke unto Abraham his father, "Father you have the wood and fire, but where is the lamb for a burnt offering?" [64] "Don't worry son, God will provide a lamb for a burnt offering," responded Abraham to him. So they came together to the place God had told him and Abraham built an altar there and laid the

---

[62] Genesis 22:4-5
[63] Genesis 22:6
[64] Genesis 22:7

wood in order, and bound Isaac his son and laid him on the altar upon the wood.

Isaac asked his father where the lamb is, and Abraham replied, that God himself would provide. That is the key and success of man's redemption... God will provide the lamb himself. It is not what man provides or offers; it is what God does. Here is an exhibition of Calvary and a new experience for Isaac. He had experienced circumcision, now he must lay down his life.

The details were as follows: At the appointed place - Calvary, God's appointed place. Abraham built an altar - Calvary was Christ's altar. Isaac bound and laid on the Altar - Christ bound to the Cross. Isaac set down upon the wood on the altar - Christ was laid upon and nailed to the wooden Cross. Isaac was obedient unto death - Christ was obedient unto death - Philippians 2:8.

And Abraham stretched forth his hand and took the knife to slay his son. And the angel of the Lord called unto him out of heaven, and said, "Abraham, Abraham. Lay not your hand upon the lad, for now I know you fear God seeing you have not withheld your son, your only son from me." And Abraham lifted up his eyes, and looked and he saw a ram caught in a thicket by his horns. He took the ram and offered him up for a burnt offering instead of his son. [65]

Abraham demonstrated that God came before the child he cherished. It was no easy act; Abraham wanted to die rather than see Isaac die. He did not know why God tested him in such an exacting way. He knew that he must trust him whatever the cost. A

---

[65] Genesis 22:10-13

51

person who does not accept and understand the redemption plan would dismiss it as weird, fantastic and foolish, but faith pleases God, and there is more to this strange event than what first meets the eyes. Sure enough God provided an offering, a ram caught in the thicket. Nobody provided the ram; God arranged it, likewise he arranged the ultimate sacrifice Christ himself.

And Abraham called the name of that place *Yahweh Jireh*, as it is said to this day, in the mount of the Lord it shall be seen. And the angel of the Lord called unto Abraham out of heaven the second time, and said, "By myself have I sworn says the Lord, because you have done this thing and did not withhold your son, your only son, in blessing I will bless you and in multiplying I will multiply your seed as the stars of the heaven and as the sand which is upon the sea shore. And your seed shall possess the gate of his enemies; and in your seed shall all the nations of the earth be blessed because you have obeyed my voice. [66]

Who is the seed that will bless all nations of the earth? It cannot be the modern nation of Israel because the Scripture talks specifically of one single seed descended from Abraham through Isaac. Paul points this out: Just because they are the seed of Abraham does not make them all children of God, but, it is through Isaac that your seed shall be called - Romans 9:7. Now to Abraham and his seed were the promises made. He did not say, to many descendants, it was only the one seed, which is Christ - Galatians 3:16.

---

[66] Genesis 22:14-18

Why did Isaac remain passive when he learned his father intended to slay him, after all, it seemed bizarre? Isaac, though in his teens, knew the Canaanites practiced child sacrifices. When he found himself a victim it must have puzzled him that Yahweh suddenly imitated the Canaanite religions and requested human sacrifices.

Machpelah

Sarah had experienced many marvelous things in her lifetime: first she grew up in the great metropolis Ur of the Chaldees; later she moved to another great city known as [67]Haran; from there she and Abram migrated to Canaan living as nomadic herders. Life was free and interesting; but she had caused a sensation both in Egypt and in Philistia; she also witnessed the smoke rise up from Sodom like a furnace; and finally, she gave birth to Isaac and shared thirty-seven fulfilled years with him.

And Sarah died in Kirjatharba, the same is Hebron in the land of Canaan, and Abraham mourned for Sarah and wept for her.[68] When Abraham migrated to Canaan God promised him the whole land yet despite his promise Abraham's testimony on the death of his wife stated that he lived as a stranger in the land. In the sixty-two years in Canaan, he never assimilated with them. Surprisingly, Abraham and Sarah did not own one foot of land to call their own. The Hethites had a communal respect for Abraham, recognized his

---

[67] Also known as Mari.
[68] Genesis 23:2

princely qualities, and wanted to give him a plot of land to bury Sarah. However, Abraham did not accept a gravesite for his wife or himself for free, he insisted on paying the full value. Abraham the father of faith paid the cost for a burial site in Canaan.

Canaan exemplifies two things: life and death. There is a cost to life and there is a cost to death. David declined Ornan the Jebusite's offer to donate his threshing-floor plot of land for the proposed temple site; David insisted on paying the full price. He said, "Shall I offer to the Lord that which costs me nothing[69]?" David paid six hundred gold shekels for it, which proved to be an expensive piece of real estate. [70] Ornan was either an extremely generous man or extremely foolish man; or maybe he felt afraid of David and made his generous offer on that basis. But David didn't personally pay for the land, his kingdom paid for it. It is interesting that God chose the [71]Canaanite Ornan's property for his Temple site.

Abraham only ever owned one piece of land in the whole of Canaan and that was his gravesite. Sometimes we cannot see the fulfilment of God's promises, but Abraham did not drown himself in reflection of what might have been or how things should be, he did what had to be done as a pledge of faith in God and God honored him for it.

Machpelah in the Hebrew language means double; Abraham experienced the double cost of faith in the land of Canaan. There is a physical death and there is a dying to oneself and all the aspirations that one possesses. God had previously said to Abraham: "I

---

[69] 1Chronicles 21:24-25

[70] Also called Araunah.

[71] Ornan was Jebusite not Israelite.

am thy reward." A life of faith is not about land titles or gold, it is about being made in his likeness and for his pleasure.

Isaac's Bride

Abraham appointed his chief servant to search out and find a bride for his son Isaac. The servant is not specifically named but is generally considered Eliezer. The commission specified an ethnic relation of Abraham. Eliezer's worried the woman would not be willing to come back with him to Canaan. Abraham had stressed Isaac must not leave Canaan so if the woman refused the journey, Eliezer would be clear from the oath.

When Eliezer finally reached Haran in Mesopotamia, the city appeared to be relatively small, at least judging by the custom of women coming outside the city to draw water from a well. It later developed into the great city of Mari and dated between 2000 and 1700 BC. The palace of the Kings of Mari covered acres of ground. An excavated Temple of Dagan, associated with the Philistines is there as well as a great Ziggurat. The Amorite inhabitants of Haran also worshipped Ishtar the fertility goddess. Mari had a complex system of irrigation, canals, locks, and dams.

Eliezer rested at the well of the city and immediately prayed, and straight away circumstances fell into place, for the young virgin [72] Rebekah came along. Eliezer prayed specifically that Isaac's potential bride would give him water to drink and offer to refresh his

---

[72] Rebekah or Rebecca in English, means captivating.

55

camels as well, so he approached Rebekah and she spontaneously offered him a drink and offered to water the camels as well. Such a quick answer to prayer elated and encouraged him.

Rebekah demonstrated a great deal of hospitality that has been lost over the millenniums of mankind. Eliezer questioned if his prayer had been answered, nevertheless he placed a golden earring upon her and put gold bracelets upon her hands and then asked about her family. To his delight, he discovered she came from the family of Abraham. Rebekah, obviously overcome by the beautiful gifts ran off to tell her family about the stranger and strange event that had just taken place. Her brother Laban ran out to show the guest the way to the house. At Bethuel's house Eliezer shared his story and asked for Rebekah's hand in marriage to Isaac, which Bethuel, Abraham's brother and the family agreed.

The western marriage proposal is generally agreed upon because of a romantic relationship and then a decision is made. Surely, Rebekah and her family took a risk; this son of Abraham may be a deplorable person. However, they made their judgment because of the character of the servant whom they met face to face; he represented the quality of the young man offered to Rebekah.

Eliezer appeared compelling nevertheless he imparted assuring confidence so that neither Rebekah nor her family could decline; the overwhelming sense of ineluctable destiny prevailed. God pre-ordained it. Upon acceptance more gifts representing the dowry, were given to Rebekah and her family. What a different scenario in Haran from that of the State sponsored seizures of Sarah in Egypt and Rebekah in

Gerar. The culture and protocols of the Hebrews in Haran suggests women had a voice in their personal matters; ultimately, Rebekah made the decision. This culture and mind-set appears more civilized than many cultures in the world today. And what a big decision for Rebekah to marry a stranger; she had heard about Isaac and knew she was related, but this decision required her to forsake her family, friends, and country, and never return. Would she venture forth on this strange journey to Canaan? She accepted.

Her family prophesied and prayed a visionary prayer for her: "Be the mother of thousands of millions; let your seed possess the gate of those that hate you." Today we usually settle for words like 'good health and prosperity,' but this blessing surpassed normal wishes. It claimed abundant, universal and creative blessing. The young Rebekah went about her domestic chores without any idea that destiny stood by waiting to transport her into the redemption plan of mankind.

Isaac meanwhile, went out into the field at eventide to meditate; he possibly still grieved the passing of his mother and no doubt felt emptiness. Isaac had no idea who Rebekah was or what she looked like, but at the exact moment that he lifted his eyes, he saw her approaching. Co-incidentally, Rebekah looked up, their eyes met and both felt the enchantment of the moment. "Who is that man?" She asked. Eliezer replied, "It is the master." She covered her face with a veil and approached as a bride.

There is something unique and special about Isaac: a man of peace, of prayer, and of meditation. When Rebekah first saw Isaac, he was in the field meditating. Isaac embodied a Christ likeness: Rebekah sensed his special quality, yet he had a romantic side to him and he cherished Rebekah who filled the gap left in his life when his mother died. Isaac loved family, his mother and father, and his sons. In contrast to others in the Bible, he only had one wife. But he grieved at the waywardness of his son, and he could not endure the heathen wives whom Esau married; they caused grief of mind and bitterness of spirit to Isaac and Rebekah, and thus he commanded Jacob that he must not marry a heathen wife.

Keturah

Then Abraham took a wife named Keturah.[73] Keturah is referred to as Abraham's [74] concubine in scripture. She may have been married to Abraham while Sarah was still alive. Her ethnic origins are unknown but she was not a slave like Hagar. God's plans involved Abraham and Isaac therefore Keturah is incidental to the story, but she was a provision from God and comforted Abraham after Sarah's death. It is ironic that Abraham spent most of his life desiring an heir; finally, at one hundred years of age when it seemed all too late, Isaac was born. However, when Keturah appears, Abraham produced a team of sons with no agonizing complications like those involved in Isaacs's conception. The way of faith is an unconventional plane.

The sons by Keturah were a bonus to Abraham, a sort of harvest after the first fruits, which was Isaac. Keturah means incense or fragrant one; judging by the amount of children she produced, indeed she proved

[73] Genesis 25:1
[74] 1Chronicles 1:32.

exactly that to Abraham. She produced the following sons for Abraham: Zimran and Jokshan, and Medan, and Midian, and Ishbak, and Shuah. Incidentally, Jokshan had Sheba and Dedan. And the sons of Dedan were Asshurim, Letushim, and Leummim. And the sons of Midian: Ephah, and Epher, and Hanoch, and Abidah, and Eldaah. All these were the children of Keturah.[75] Josephus claims these sons were 'men of courage and sagacious minds' and that one of the sons of Midian, Epher, made war against Libya and took it; and that his grandchildren called it from his name - Africa.

Isaac's uniqueness is obvious among the sons of Abraham for he inherited the Promised Land. The other sons from Keturah were sent away eastward; they did not go out empty handed for Abraham rewarded them individually.

Apart from Epher pronounced as – Afer, from whom the name Africa derives, the other name that stands out is Midian. Israel appeared surrounded by relations: Uncle Lot's sons Moab and Ammon; Esau's country Edom; and Midian and Ishmael. An intimate connection existed between Israel and a branch of Midian that endured throughout the ages. Moses married Zipporah a Midianite. Her father Jethro and Moses had a lasting friendship. Jethro's tribal branch was known as the Kenites. The Midianites figure prominently in Old Testament and were not always benevolent to Israel.

The women who figured prominently in the Patriarch's life represent principles and lessons for Believers. Sarah for example typified the promise of Grace; Hagar, on the other hand typified the Law; whereas Keturah typified fruits of faith, for Abraham

---

[75] Genesis 25:2-4

was the father of faith. Believers or children of father Abraham have their Keturah experiences with their multiplicity of fruits produced by faith. Things like impressive church buildings and missions of all varieties. But these things cannot remain alongside of Isaac, they must be sent away so that they do not corrupt Isaac's inheritance. Alas many Christians get caught up in great projects which are human occupations and fruits of faith but not Christ himself, and these things can corrupt the inheritance of Christ in Believers' lives.

Abraham's Eulogy

These are the years of Abraham's life, which he lived, one hundred and seventy five years. Abraham died an old man and full of years. He was gathered to his people and his sons Isaac and Ishmael buried him in the cave of Machpelah in the field of Ephron the son of Zohar the Hittite, which is before Mamre; the field that Abraham purchased from the sons of Heth. Both Abraham and Sarah his wife are buried there. [76]

Abraham's final resting place was beside his wife Sarah at Machpelah; it was the only plot of land that Abraham ever purchased.

---

[76] Genesis 25:7-10

Chronology Chart/Bible Genealogical table*

(Dates approximate only)

2662: Eber*
2600: Building of Pyramids
2528: Phaleg*
2528: Dispersion of nations\Peleg-division*
2500: Building of Mohenjo-daro, Indus basin.
2500: Andean Civilization
2400: Aryan migration
2398: Ragau*
2371: Sargon founds Akkad Agade period.
2266: Serug*
2230: Hebron founded.
2223: Founding of Memphis.
2205: Chinese civilization
2200: Middle Minoan pottery; linear writing in pen and ink.
2136: Nahor*
2113: 3rd dynasty of Ur.
2107: Terah*
2100: Building of Stonehenge?
2165-1990: Abram, Higher Chronology. Genesis 11:31.
2080: Assyrians: Amraphel, Arioch, Chedolaomer and Tidal, capture the five kings of the Sodom plain; Balas, Barsas, Senabar, Sumobor and the King of Bela called Zoar.
2080: Abram and Melchizedek King of Salem.
2060: Sodom and Gomorrah destroyed
2037: Abram*
2000: Minoan settlements in Aegean; Indonesian settlement?

2065-1885: Isaac
2000-1860: Jacob
2000-1000: Middle & Late Bronze Age.
2000: Use of Iron
2000: Rise of Babylon
2000: Bronze Age in Europe
2000: Jomons settle Japan
1962: Amenemmes I, 12th Dynasty middle kingdom
1962: Another possible date for Abram coming out
of Haran.
1928: Sesostris I
1910-1800: Joseph
1875: Jacob. Approximate Entry into Egypt
1894-1595: Old Babylonian period 1st dynasty
of Babylon.
1895: Amenemmes II
1878: Sesostris II
1843: Sesostris III
1800-1760: Hammurabi Babylon/Mari
1786: 13th to 17th Dynasty, 2nd Intermediate
period. Josephus claims Hyksos Phoenician shepherds
controlled and departed Egypt before the Israelites
sojourn.
1751: Hammurabi code at Babylon

Endnotes

Scriptures are based mainly on the Authorized Version (AV) or my own translations and paraphrases from the original languages. I have used US spelling.

This story continues in: Isaac - Son of Abraham
(Genesis - The Bible Study)
Amazon
ISBN-10: 1490324550
ISBN-13: 978-1490324555

Made in the USA
Middletown, DE
05 March 2017